Lucinda sat at the airport feeling very overwhelmed. She was about to board a plane for the first time in her life.

Her family was moving from Mexico to Canada
because her dad had gotten a new job.
Her mother, brother and sister were all excited
because they wanted to go to a new country,
but she was terrified.

Everything would be so new to her. She was leaving behind her friends, her cousins and her grandparents whom she loved dearly and this made her very sad.

As she got on the plane, she began to feel claustrophobic. It looked so big from the outside but inside, it was small and cramped. Lucinda really did not want to leave her home, but she had no choice in the matter.

She closed her eyes as the plane took off
and before she knew it, she was fast asleep.

When she woke up, the plane was about
to descend at the airport.
It was nighttime so she could see all the
beautiful lights of the city below.
It was quite spectacular.

On arriving, Lucinda and her family went to
an apartment which was her new home.
It was so different from what she was
accustomed to. She never had to use an elevator
to get to her house in Mexico. When she looked
down from her apartment, it was quite
scary. It felt like she was living in the sky.

Lucinda was very nervous to start school.
Her English was not very good, and she
was worried about fitting in
with the other students.

On her first day of school, she walked slowly to her classroom, dreading being the new girl. Her teacher, Mr. Clarke, was very welcoming and nice. He included her in all activities and tried to make her feel comfortable.

However, no one else spoke to her. The other students simply ignored her. She ate lunch alone and sat on a bench close to the playground watching the other students play tag.

No one invited her to join the game and being shy, she didn't make the effort to ask to play. She was also afraid that they would be mean to her and mock her poor English.

One day, Mr. Clarke asked each student to talk about their favourite place to visit. When it was Lucinda's turn, she knew what she wanted to say but could not remember the English word for "beach".

She started her sentence with "I like to go to"
and paused. She repeated it again but
was still having difficulty. Eventually
she said, " I like to go to la playa."

Some of the kids laughed and
Mr. Clarke immediately intervened.

He told Lucinda that he was so glad that she tried her best and gave her some markers and paper to draw a picture so he could understand what she was referring to.

Lucinda initially felt embarrassed standing in front of the class but Mr. Clarke was very supportive. She sat down, drew a beautiful picture of the beach and gave it to Mr. Clarke.

He smiled and told her that he was learning from her because he did not know any Spanish. He later took her drawing and stuck it on the bulletin board outside of the classroom.

Lucinda had a talent for drawing, and she spent most of her time doing this. Ms. Ramsay, the art teacher, saw Lucinda's work on the board and asked her to join the art club. Lucinda was elated and quickly accepted the opportunity.

The days passed by, and nothing changed. She disliked going to school because she didn't have any friends. Lucinda wanted to return to Mexico where she was happy and carefree and could speak Spanish without being worried or fearful of being ridiculed by others.

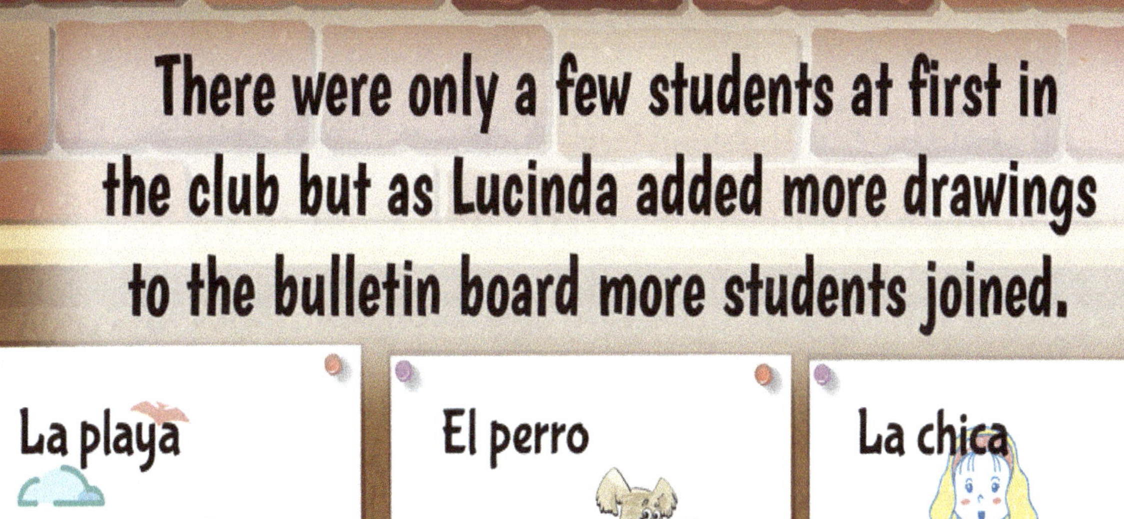

There were only a few students at first in the club but as Lucinda added more drawings to the bulletin board more students joined.

They admired her work and complimented her on being an incredible artist. She labelled each of her drawings in Spanish and soon the bulletin board was covered with new words. She was surrounded by so many students who were interested in learning her language and she felt so proud.

Lucinda helped the students at her school with
Spanish and told them all about her life in Mexico.
She was so happy to share her experiences
with them and in turn, her English
was improving tremendously.

Her days at school were now filled with joy and laughter and every evening, she couldn't wait to tell her parents how much fun she had with her new friends.

Although she missed Mexico a lot, Lucinda was finally starting to settle in her new home, and she knew that everything was going to be just alright.